Elephants

General Editor
Tim Harris

BROWN BEAR BOOKS

Published by Brown Bear Books Ltd

4877 N. Circulo Bujia
Tucson, AZ 85718
USA

and

First Floor
9-17 St. Albans Place
London N1 0NX

© 2012 Brown Bear Books Ltd

ISBN: 978-1-78121-003-1

Managing Editor: Tim Harris
Designer: Lynne Lennon
Picture Manager: Sophie Mortimer
Art Director: Jeni Child
Production Director: Alastair Gourlay
Editorial Director: Lindsey Lowe
Children's Publisher: Anne O'Daly

Library of Congress Cataloging-in-Publication Data available upon request

Publisher's note to educators and parents: Our editors have carefully reviewed the websites that appear on p. 31 to ensure that they are suitable for students. Many websites change frequently, however, and we cannot guarantee that a site's future contents will continue to meet our high standards of quality and educational value. Be advised that students should be closely supervised whenever they access the Internet.

Manufactured in the United States of America

Contents

Introduction

Elephants are the biggest and strongest of all land-living animals. With their trunks, tusks, and giant ears, they look like no other animal.

As well as being powerful, elephants are intelligent. They have large brains that grow through youth, making them very good at learning. In fact, they display some behaviors seen in few other animals.

Elephants are mammals, like we are. They make caring mothers, showing great care toward their young. There are two different types (species) of elephants. One type lives in Africa, and the other lives in Asia.

The African elephant is the largest land animal. Its long trunk and large ears make it unmistakable.

Using tools

Elephants often use tools. Wild elephants have been seen using twigs and branches to brush away flies or scratch themselves. Elephants are the only animals apart from monkeys and other primates that can throw things. Using their trunk like an arm, they sometimes pick up objects and hurl them at other animals or people.

Elephants are social animals. They all spend at least part of their lives in groups. Some elephants never leave the groups they were born into.

In this book you will learn all about how elephants live together. Later on you will find out more about just what makes them such special animals.

This Asian elephant has just used its trunk to suck up some water for a drink.

The elephant's trunk

An elephant's trunk is a combination of its nose and its upper lip. It contains lots of different muscles, making it flexible and easy to maneuver. Elephants use their trunks to pick up food, suck up water, caress one another, fight, smell, and make trumpeting calls.

Elephant herds

Most elephants live in groups called herds. The basic elephant herd is an extended family of female elephants and their young.

Adult male (called bull) elephants usually live alone, but sometimes they live in temporary herds of their own. They only join the female herds when they are looking for a mate. The females in the basic elephant herd are always related. They spend their whole lives together, and the bonds between them are strong. They help each other raise and protect the young, they travel together, and they feed as a group. Herd members rarely move more than 50 yards (15m) apart.

Big and small herds

African elephant herds range from two to about 24 animals. Sometimes herds of related female elephants join to form groups of 50 or so members, called clans. Asian elephants have smaller herds of usually ten or fewer animals. If herds get too big, they split in two.

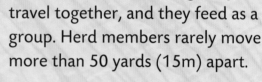

↶ Female elephants with their calves. Most females in a herd are related, and they help each other care for the young.

These herds often meet, with a lot of excitement and friendly trumpeting noises. Elephant herds do not always stay in the same place, but each does have certain areas where it can often be found. These areas may be shared with other herds.

The leader of the herd

The leader of the herd is the matriarch. She is the oldest and largest female. She makes decisions that affect the others. The matriarch leads the herd to find new feeding grounds. When she stops to feed, the rest of the herd stops with her.

Adult and calf Asian elephants have a cooling bathe in a river. Bathing is a favorite activity for elephants.

Washing off and dusting down

Elephants enjoy bathing. When they reach a river or watering hole, they often wade right in before even taking a drink. Bathing cleans the skin and cools the elephants. It also gives youngsters an excuse to play.

Staying in touch

Elephants are great communicators. With their trunks and huge ears they have very good senses of smell and hearing. They use both to keep in touch.

Elephants can "talk" to each other over very long distances. They can send messages across several miles (kilometers) using infrasound (see the box). They use normal sound and infrasound to communicate at closer range.

Body language

When they can see each other, elephants use body language, touch, and smell much more. The ears are used like flags. They are spread out to show aggression or dominance and flattened back against the head to indicate submission or fear. The trunk is also used for communication. When two elephants meet

➔ Two male elephants greet each other by gently touching their trunks.

after being apart, one puts its trunk into the other's mouth as a greeting. Swinging the trunk forward is a threat. Mothers comfort their infants by touching them with their trunks.

Elephants have a very good sense of smell. They raise their trunks and sniff the air to get information about their surroundings. They recognize different members of the herd by their odor, and they can smell elephants from outside the herd too. They may even be able to tell when another elephant is becoming excited or angry by changes in its odor.

Jungle rumbles

As well as making trumpeting noises, elephants use very low-pitched sounds, called infrasound, to "talk" to each other. Infrasound is too low-pitched for humans to hear ("infra" means below). But for a large animal like an elephant the sound is easy to pick up. Elephants use infrasound to communicate over long distances.

◐ Communication is an important part of elephant society. It helps adults and calves stay together.

Getting enough to eat

An fully grown bull African elephant can weigh 8 tons (7.3 tonnes)—the weight of 100 people. That makes finding enough food each day a full-time job.

An adult male elephant eats up to 350 pounds (159kg) of plant matter every day. He can spend 18 hours a day looking for it. At least an elephant can eat a wide range of plants. This helps because it means the animal can feed at many different levels.

Having a long trunk makes it easy for elephants to reach up high for food. They also pick up fallen fruit from the ground.

Drinking

Elephants drink a lot of water. An adult African elephant can drink up to 50 gallons (190 l) a day. An elephant sucks water into its trunk then squirts it into its mouth. Herds usually travel to water at least once a day but can go without it for two weeks.

◀ Elephants prefer some watering holes to others. They choose those with high amounts of minerals in the water.

Using its trunk, it can tear grass from the ground or reach up to strip leaves from the high branches of trees. It can also rip away tree bark that it has loosened with its tusks.

Eat, eat, eat

Once it has grasped the food with its trunk, an elephant passes the food up to its mouth. There, four huge teeth called molars (two in each jaw) crush and grind the food before the animal swallows. Food takes between 22 and 46 hours to pass through the body as dung. Elephant dung provides food for many smaller animals and is also excellent fertilizer for the soil.

Elephants need so much food that they spend nearly every waking hour feeding. The herd munches through much of the day and most of the night as well. True sleep is just two or three hours around the hottest time of the day or just after midnight.

The mating game

When they are about 10 or 11 years old, female elephants are able to mate. When she is able to mate, a female elephant is said to be "in estrus."

Females in estrus attract nearby males to mate with them. When a female starts to come into estrus, she often walks in an unusual way. She holds her head high and looks back over her shoulders. This is called an estrus walk, and it may help draw males to her. Females in estrus also make special sounds. Some of these sounds can be heard by humans; others are too low. These sounds may help attract roaming males.

A bull elephant "in must" dribbles oily liquid from glands behind his eyes.

Males "in must"

About once every year adult bull elephants go through a change in their behavior known as must. Must is caused by increased levels of the male hormone, testosterone. Bulls "in must" are much more aggressive than usual, and other bulls usually keep away from them. But sometimes two must bulls meet. When this happens, they fight.

A male and a female Asian elephant twist their trunks around each other. They do this before they mate.

Before mating takes place

Once she has attracted a bull elephant, the female usually urinates. She does this so that the male can smell the odor of her urine. The odor tells the bull whether the female is really ready to mate or not. If she is ready, he becomes excited. The female walks quickly away, and the bull chases after her. Female elephants are quicker than males, so if she is not impressed by her partner, she can easily get away from him. If she does like him, she will let him catch up with her, and the pair will then mate. The largest bull elephants are most popular with females. Bull elephants that are in must are always chosen rather than those that are not in must.

Asian elephants have a slightly different mating behavior from African elephants. Asian elephants stand face to face and twine their trunks together before they mate.

Bringing up the calves

Baby elephants, or calves, can walk within an hour, but they are very shaky on their feet for the first few days. The mother stays close to her baby.

The mother feeds the young elephant on her milk and protects it from enemies for the first year of its life. The other females in the herd help with bringing up baby. If the mother is separated from her calf for any reason, one of the other females rushes to its side to comfort it. These elephant "aunts" will even let a youngster comfort-suckle.

Play time

When they are not feeding or traveling with the herd, baby elephants spend a lot of time playing. They charge playfully at smaller animals, birds, and bushes, and they jostle with each other.

Young males spend a lot of time wrestling and

◑ Elephant calves spend much of their time playing—particularly with each other.

Growing up

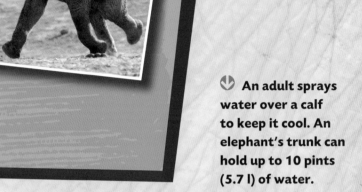

Baby elephants start off big and then just get bigger. A newborn African elephant weighs about 265 pounds (120kg). By the time it is six years old, it tips the scales at a ton (0.9 tonnes).

An adult sprays water over a calf to keep it cool. An elephant's trunk can hold up to 10 pints (5.7 l) of water.

chasing one another around. As they get older, they find new partners for these games. By the time they are six or seven years old they start leaving the herd for short periods. They search for different families to find males of a similar age to play-fight with.

Young females

Young females gradually grow out of play. At five or six years old they start helping to care for the smallest babies. They keep an eye on them while the mother is busy and sometimes guard them while they sleep.

Male Elephants

Young male elephants start to become adults when they are about 12. Their play gets more aggressive, and they spend more time away from the herd.

Young males finally leave the herd when they are 15 or 16. As they get more aggressive, the older females lose patience. Eventually the females drive the young elephants away from the herd. Once they have left, male elephants behave in different ways. Some wander by themselves, while others form all-male groups. A few join a different family

Two bulls clash in a head-to-head fight. A battle between bulls can last up to six hours!

herd. They stay with it for up to a year then go off on their own.

While they are in their late teens and early twenties, bull elephants keep the herding instinct. They join large groups of females for short periods or travel with other bulls. All-male herds are good places for the younger bull elephants to test out their strength.

All by himself

Fully grown bulls wander from herd to herd, particularly when they are looking for a female to mate with. As bull elephants get older, they spend more time on their own. The oldest bulls usually live alone. Most stay near swamps where there is water and vegetation soft enough to chew with their worn-out teeth.

⬆ **Adult male elephants spend some time with a herd and some time alone.**

Aggressive behavior

Male elephants fight from an early age. Even as babies they find youngsters of a similar size to tussle with. As they get older, their fighting gets more serious. Bulls joining an all-male group wrestle with the others to establish their rank. Bulls battling to mate with a female may even fight to the death. Some males test their strength by toppling trees over!

Female elephants

Females spend their whole lives in the family groups they were born into. When they are a few years old, they play less and help out more.

Eventually, female elephants attract the attention of adult males. Females first mate when they are 10 or 11 years old. Once she has mated, a female carries her unborn baby growing inside her for more than 22 months. The bonding between females in the elephant herd is strong. Most herds are extended family groups, and all the females in them are

⚲ **Adult elephants gather around calves to protect them when danger threatens.**

closely related. Because they are all either mothers, daughters, sisters, or cousins of one another, they work together to look after the young.

A mother stays close to her calf for the whole of its first year. Other females will also help out.

The protection of the herd

When a mother is busy feeding, a younger female watches over her baby to make sure it does not get into difficulties. And when faced by a predator, the whole herd forms a wall of trunks and legs to shield the infants. It must be a menacing sight for a would-be attacker.

Female elephants never grow as big as the adult males, nor do they grow such long tusks. Female Asian elephants hardly have tusks at all.

Birth

Females have their first baby when they are 12 or 13. Some give birth surrounded by the rest of the herd. Others leave for a short while to have the baby alone. Elephants give birth standing up, so babies have a big drop to the ground!

19

When elephants grow old and die

Elephants are among the longest-lived of all animals. Wild African elephants can easily reach 60 years old, and wild Asian elephants may live to 70.

Because of their size adult elephants have very few predators. Diseases kill some elephants when they are still young, but many live to old age. Starvation is the main natural killer of elephants. Every elephant gets six sets of bricklike molar teeth in its lifetime. Once the sixth set has worn out, the elephant can no longer feed, so it starves to death.

Poaching and shooting

Apart from starvation the main killer of elephants is humans. Many African elephants never get to reach a natural death. One reason for this is because they are poached for their ivory tusks.

These playful young elephants could live for another 50 years or more.

Several African elephants sniff the bones of a dead elephant.

Another reason is that some are shot to prevent their numbers growing too large. Asian elephants are not hunted in the same way, so most live to old age.

Understanding death?

Elephants do some things that suggest they may understand death. Whenever they come across dead elephants, they become excited. They explore the bones with their trunks and even pick them up.

Elephant graves

There are places where lots of elephant skeletons have been found together. Sick and dying elephants usually go to areas where there is plenty of food and water. The elephants die there, and their bones collect over the years.

There are places like this in Africa and Asia where elephants go to die.

Ears, tusks, and trunks

With its long trunk, enormous ears, and tusks an elephant looks like nothing else on Earth. Each of these strange things has an important job to do.

Why are an elephant's ears so big? The main reason is that they help elephants cool down. Each ear is filled with hundreds of blood vessels. As the blood flows through the vessels in the ear, heat escapes through the skin into the surrounding air. When the weather is really hot, elephants flap their ears, which helps them lose heat even more quickly.

Strong teeth

The tusks are giant incisor teeth. Elephants use their tusks to pull up roots, tear the bark off trees, and dig out waterholes. They also use their tusks as weapons. Elephants come in different sizes. An adult bull African bush elephant may weigh 7 tons (6.4 tonnes) and stand 12 feet (3.6 m) tall.

It is easy to tell an Asian elephant, such as this one, from its African cousin. Asian elephants have smaller ears and a domed head. Their bodies are smaller and chunkier.

⬇ An African bush elephant's ears make up one seventh of its body surface.

Trunks

An African elephant has two "fingers" at the end of its trunk (left), while an Asian elephant has one (right).

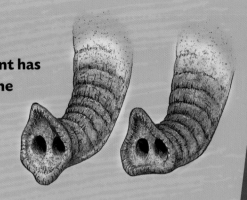

Elephant ancestors

Elephants have lived on Earth for around 50 million years. The earliest elephant (*Moenitherium*) was about the size of a pig and had no trunk.

It was another 15 million years before creatures that we might recognize as elephants first appeared. *Phimia* lived 35 million years ago. This early elephant had a short trunk and tusks coming from both its upper and lower jaws.

Mastadons and mammoths

One of the later elephant species was *Platybelodon*. This strange-looking creature lived about 20 million years ago in marshy areas. It used its shovel-shaped teeth to dig up vegetation. Another early elephant was the now-extinct mastodon. Mastodons looked like the modern Asian elephant and the woolly mammoth, but they were not closely related to them. Mastodons first appeared long before either mammoths or modern elephants evolved.

⬇ **The earliest elephants looked nothing like their modern relatives. As elephants evolved (changed over time), they began to look more like the animals we know today. They developed trunks and tusks.**

Moenitherium

Phimia

The woolly mammoth was a large elephant with long, sharply curved tusks. It was covered with a shaggy coat of hair to keep it warm in the frozen lands where it lived. Our own ancestors hunted woolly mammoths for food until they died out about 10,000 years ago. Mammoths were more closely related to the Asian elephant than the African elephant is!

Elephants in America

Today, elephants are found only in Africa and Asia. But once there were relatives of elephants in America. Mammoths and mastodons lived in America until about 10,000 years ago. Mammoths lived mainly on the plains and mastodons mainly in the forests. They died out because the climate and plantlife changed and also because people hunted them.

Hyraxes are among elephants' closest living relatives. They are rabbit-sized animals with hooves.

Platybelodon

Mammoth

Elephant habitats

Elephants live in a variety of different types of environment. The African savanna elephant lives mostly on dry open plains and in open woodland.

The African forest elephant and Asian elephant are creatures of thick tropical forests. Elephants are tough animals. In Africa they live in scorching desert and near the chilly peaks of mountains as high as 15,000 ft (4,572m). All they need to survive is enough food to eat and water to drink.

Africa and Asia

In the fairly recent past African elephants roamed across the whole of Africa south of the Sahara Desert. They followed ancient paths in search of food and water. Asian elephants lived

Shrinking homelands

The main threat to elephants in the wild is habitat destruction. As the human population has grown, so has the demand for farmland. In India and China, for example, there are few wild places left.

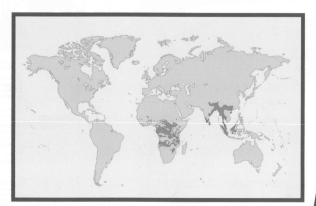

⬆ **The forests where Asian elephants live are often needed for farmland. Each year there is less land for the elephants.**

⬇ **A herd of African elephants near the great peak of Kilimanjaro in Tanzania, eastern Africa.**

from the Middle East through Pakistan and India to Borneo and north into China.

Farms or elephants?

Clearing the land to grow crops and build houses (habitat destruction) has reduced the area in which both African and Asian elephants can live. Hunting has also reduced the ranges of both species. However, they are still fairly widespread.

The African elephant still lives in 35 of Africa's 42 countries. In Asia east of Pakistan the Asian elephant lives in parts of every country apart from Taiwan, Korea, Japan, and the Philippines.

People and elephants

People and elephants have worked closely together for thousands of years. The Asian elephant in particular has a long history with humans.

Elephants are intelligent animals and can be trained to do all sorts of things. In the past huge numbers of Asian elephants were used in the logging industry. Despite the development of bulldozers and other machinery, thousands of elephants are still used today. The elephant's combination of great strength and nimble feet make it ideal for this heavy work.

An elephant at the Songkran festival in Bangkok, Thailand, squirts water over some surprised onlookers.

Hannibal's elephants

The African elephant is almost unknown as a domestic animal, and many people believe that it cannot be tamed. However, records show that as long ago as 217 B.C.E. African forest elephants were used as beasts of war. The famous Carthaginian leader Hannibal used the elephants to cross the mountains of the Alps in Europe.

Elephants in zoos

In the western world today elephants are seen mostly in zoos and circuses. Keeping elephants properly requires lots of space, which is something that most zoos and circuses do not have.

Asian elephants are put to work hauling logs in the logging industry. These elephants in Thailand are giving a demonstration of their amazing strength.

India's elephants

Of all the countries in the world, India has the closest ties to elephants. They are painted and ridden in processions and festivals. They carry tourists through national parks and roam wild in forests. The Hindu religion says they even live in the heavens.

Glossary

ancestors Animals from which elephants have developed over a very long period of time.

bull elephant An adult male elephant.

habitat The kinds of places where a particular animal lives, such as a forest or a desert.

herd A group of elephants. Most herds are made up of related females and their young, but males sometimes form their own herds. A superherd is a collection of many elephants from several herds that meet where there is lots of food to eat. A superherd contains both male and female elephants.

infrasound Noises that are too low-pitched for humans to hear but which can be made and heard by elephants.

mammal A kind of animal that is warm-blooded and has a backbone. Most mammals are covered with fur.

Female mammals have glands that produce milk to feed their young.

matriarch The oldest and largest female; the leader of the herd.

molar A large tooth used for grinding.

must A temporary change in the behavior of adult male elephants that makes them more aggressive.

testosterone A chemical called a hormone that bull elephants produce when they go into must.

trumpeting The loud noise made by elephants.

trunk A combination of an elephant's nose and upper lip. It is used to pick up food, suck up water, and to smell.

tusk Two giant teeth at the front of the mouth used for digging, pulling, and fighting. Elephants are still hunted for their valuable ivory tusks, although the practice is illegal.

Further Reading

Books

Elephants. Francis Brennan. New York: Children's Press, 2012.

Elephants. Jacqueline Dineen. New York: Weigl, 2010.

Elephants. Jen Green. Danbury, CT: Grolier, 2009.

Elephants. Sophie Lockwood. Mankato, MN: Child's World, 2008.

Elephants. Paul May. Oxford: Oxford University Press, 2009.

Elephants. Kate Riggs. Mankato, MN: Creative, 2012.

Elephants of Africa. Gail Gibbons. New York: Holiday House, 2008.

Elephants in Danger. Helen Orme. New York: Bearport, 2007.

Secret Lives of Elephants. Julie Barnes. Milwaukee, WI: Gareth Stevens, 2007.

The Top 50 Reasons to Care about Elephants. Mary Firestone. Berkeley Heights, NJ: Enslow, 2010.

Websites

Elephant Encyclopedia
Facts and general information about elephants.
www.elephant.se

The Worldwide Fund for Nature
Topical information about elephant conservation in Africa and Asia.
www.panda.org

African Wildlife Foundation
Conservation projects for elephants and other African animals.
www.awf.org

EleAid
Lots of information about elephants and a great photo album.
www.eleaid.com

Index

The Christmas Book

COUNCIL OAK BOOKS

The Christmas Book
Council Oak Books
Tulsa / San Francisco

Originally published as *Le livre de Noël, des activités pour toute la famille* ©1997 Éditions Nathan

Council Oak Books, LLC
Tulsa, Oklahoma 74120

Editorial Direction: Catherine Faveau
Artistic Direction and Graphic Design: Claire Rébillard
Editing: Emmanuelle Fumet
Translation: Lynn Taylor

Collaborators:
Crafts artists: Béatrice Garel (40-41, 52-53, 54-55, 64-65, 82-89), Céline Markovic (20-25, 28-29, 48-49, 62-63, 66-67, 76-77), Élise Ouvrier-Buffet (26-27, 34-35, 38-39, 68-69, 74-75), Savine Pied (12-13, 18-19, 30-31, 36-37, 50-51, 58-59, 70-71), Natacha Seret (32-33, 44-45, 56-57, 72-73), Laurence Wichegrod (14-15, 42-43, 46-47, 78-79), **Photography:** Philippe Ughetto, **Styling:** Sabine Paris, **Illustrations:** Thérèse Ayrinhac and Emmanuel Cerisier, **Interior mock-up:** Isabelle Peters, Atelier Pangaud, **Text:** Emmanuelle Fumet

With the participation of Céline Lamartinie

The publisher thanks
Rougié & Plé, Lefranc and Bourgeois, for materials furnished
Geneviève Lethu, Point à la Ligne, Mokuba and B. Carant, Artgato for design work

Rougié & Plé, 13-15 bd des Filles du Calvaire, 75003 Paris

Artgato, 5 av du Docteur Arnold Netter, 75012 Paris

Photographic credits: p. 5 © AKG photo, p. 6 top © AKG photo, p. 6 middle © Jacques Guillard/Scope, p, 6 bottom © Rémi Michel/Rapho,. p. 7 top © AKG photo, p. 7 bottom © Artephot/Nimatallah, p. 8 top © J.-L. Charmet, p. 8 bottom © Andy Zito/The Image Bank, p. 10 © Christa Kieffer/The Image Bank, p. 16 © David Gould/The Image Bank, p. 60 © David Brownell/The Image Bank, p. 80 © G. de Laubier/SIP, p. 90 © E. Wallin/The Image Bank.

ISBN: 1-57178-074-2

Contents

*I*ntroduction

Christmas is a welcome break in the dull, gray winter. A promise of shared happiness and a time for families, fun, and festivities. To help get your holiday celebrations underway, this book offers dozens of simple, fun holiday activities for you and your family to participate in together.

The First Christmas

Christmas marks the celebration of the birth of Christ. The word Christmas is derived from "Christ's Mass", the special church service which celebrates the birth of the Christ child. The story of the first Christmas is told in the Gospels of Luke and Matthew. At the time of the Great Roman Empire, under the rule of Emperor Augustus, the order was given that all people were to return to the town of their birth to register for the census. In the village of Nazareth lived a carpenter, Joseph and his young wife Mary. Mary was expecting a child. She had been chosen by God to bear his son. Because of the census, Mary and Joseph had to return to Bethlehem, where Joseph was from. However, the hour of Jesus' birth came in the middle of the night and they were forced to seek shelter in a stable because there was no room in the inn. Mary gave birth to Jesus, wrapped him in swaddling clothes, and lay him in the manger.

Shepherds watching their sheep in the fields nearby saw a bright star appear in the sky. An angel came to them and announced the birth of the saviour. They followed the star to the stable where they knelt before the newborn saviour. Three kings of the Orient saw the mysterious star rise in the sky and they followed it to Bethlehem. They too knelt before Jesus offering him gifts of gold, frankincense and myrrh.

Why Celebrate Christmas on the 25th of December ?

The Bible does not give the precise date of the birth of Jesus, but it is thought to be related to the ancient celebration of the winter solstice of mid-December. The solstice gave rise to big festivals which were supposed to implore the dark days of winter and to speed the return of light. As Christianity spread throughout the Roman Empire, the church and the Christian Emperor Constantine adopted the symbolic date of December 25 as the day of the celebration of Christ's birth.

Advent

Advent lasts four weeks and ends after midnight mass on December 25th. Many people celebrate Advent by hanging holly wreaths on their front doors. Special church services are held and special Advent candles are lit each Sunday at church. Children's favorites are Advent calendars, special calendars which count down the days from December 1 until Christmas. Everday from the 1st through the 24th, a door is opened and a treat revealed.

The Crèche

Crèche is the French word for manger and both have become synonymous with the Christmas scene. It is believed that Saint Francis of Assissi came up with the idea of recreating the scene in the stable of the birth of Jesus. Still today, nativity scenes are re-enacted in many parts of the world. In many homes, miniture nativity scenes can be found during the Christmas holidays. It is often the custom to add a figure each day, ending on Christmas Eve with the baby Jesus.

The Tree

Evergreens have been a part of mid-winter festivals since long before the arrival of Christ. They played a symbolic part because they stayed green and alive when other trees appeared to be dead and bare. On the old calendar of Saints, December 24th was dedicated to the re-enactment of the creation of man. The evergreen was hung with apples and used as a substitute for the tree of creation. Since that time it has become the Christmas tree symbolizing light and salvation.

German immigrants brought with them the tradition of bringing Christmas trees into the home to decorate. Early Christmas trees were decorated with apples, nuts, cookies and candles. Then came homemade ornaments of wood, wax, glass and papier-mâché. The invention of electricity made it possible for Christmas trees to glow for days on end.

The Yule Log

In Europe the solstice celebrations were marked by the burning of the yule log. The log was cut and burned continuously for three days, sometimes until January 6, Advent. The ashes were spread about and thought to be a source of good luck for the upcoming year. The custom has changed greatly and today one eats a symbolic Yule Log Cake.

Christmas Eve

Food and drink have always been an intergal part of the Christmas Celebration. For years it has been the tradition for families to come together on Christmas Eve or Christmas day for a big feast. Today the traditional Christmas meal is varied but often includes turkey, ham, gravy, dressing, candied yams, vegetables, egg nog, and assorted cakes, pies and cookies for desert.

Epiphany

Christmas ends on January 6, the day of Epiphany which marks the presentation of Baby Jesus to the three kings. For many orthodox Christians, Advent was the actual date of the Christmas celebration. In some countries Advent is still celebrated, especially in France where a King Cake marks the day. Originally a bean was baked into the cake, but has now been replaced by a figurine. The person who finds the figurine is named King or Queen and rules over the games and celebration.

Offering Gifts

The custom of offering or exchanging gifts at the end of the year dates
back to antiquity. However, the first benefactors of this Christmas offering
were the three wise men. We have continued this gesture probably because
it so accurately reflects the the meaning of this holiday.

In Russia legend tells that on Christmas night, a little old woman,
Baboushka, refuses to accompany the three kings to Bethlehem when they
pass her door because she is too old and frail. Stricken with remorse over
her decision, she attempts to rejoin them with a basket of toys but does so
in vain. Since then it is said that she helps Father Frost make
his deliveries of toys all over Russia the night of
December 31st.

The legend of Father Christmas begins with a man called Saint Nicholas,
the Bishop of Turkey. He was one of the first bishops of the early Christian
Church and was imprisoned by the Romans because of his faith. He is
remembered for his kindness to children and is thus the patron saint of
children. Saint Nicholas is especially known in Europe where some still
celebrate Saint Nicholas' Day on December 6th. On the night of

December 5th Saint Nicholas is said to travel
by donkey delivering toys to all good
children. Father Christmas is one of the
newest recruits to the Christmas tradition and
a direct descendent of Saint Nicholas. He first
appeared in Germany in the 16th century and
then in America soon after. It is from the
Dutch Sinter Klass that we take our modern

name Santa Claus or Father Christmas. In fact it was an American, Clement Moore, who told the tale of Jolly Old Saint Nick in his poem "Twas the Night Before Christmas" which he wrote for his children in 1820. The poem detailed all the characteristics of Santa that we know today. Just like the Sinter Klass of the Netherlands, this Father Christmas filled the stockings, entered and exited through the chimney and traveled on a sleigh pulled by eight reindeer. The poem was illustrated, published and soon became popular all throughout the United States.

The Letter to Santa

Using your imagination, write a letter to Santa Claus, and decorate it with pictures and drawings. Then all you need to do is address the envelope to Santa Claus care of the North Pole, stamp it and mail it.

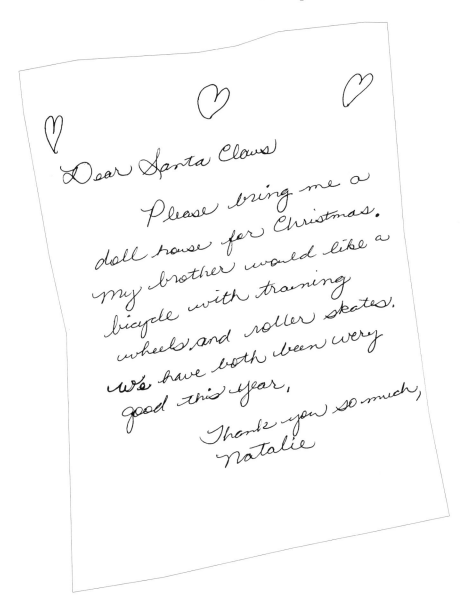

waiting for the Big day

As December comes, impatience grows.

Young and old alike anticipate the presents

and loved ones that arrive with the season.

The Advent calendar reveals its suprises

and ideas for gifts are exchanged.

The Advent Calendar

easy

inexpensive

1/2 a day

Materials

- 28 large match boxes
- packing twine • kitchen twine • 1 dozen beads
- 1 leather lace • small block of red modeling clay
- assorted colored paper
- 36" x 36" of corrugated cardboard
- 22" x 36" of poster board or tag board • packing tape
- multi-purpose glue
- a craft knife • scissors
- old magazines
- a tube of green paint
- a paint brush

1 Tape four match boxes together with packing tape, four boxes per level.

Cut out the center walls of the four center boxes, for the December 25th drawer.

Open two sides of the drawers and tape together to create one bigger.

Cut out a square of poster board with the same dimensions as the larger drawer, and twice as tall.

Glue it to the outside of the drawer. Cover all the drawers in colored paper.

2 You can make many different styles of drawer handles. Using the needle, pierce a semi-circle in the top middle section of the drawer, then cut

it out with the craft knife. Make two holes, thread a loop of the packing twine through them, then secure the ends with tape.

Make two holes, thread one or two beads through the kitchen twine, and then thread the twine through the holes. Tie a knot at the end of the twine to secure it.

Make a hole, glue the end of a piece of leather lace and stick it through the hole.

3 Cut out the numbers 1-24 from a magazine or newspaper. Glue them onto drawers. Roll out a big coil of red clay and form the number 25, flatten it and glue to the December 25th drawer.

4 Glue pieces of corrugated cardboard onto the top and sides of the match box ensemble

Glue the ensemble to a large piece of corrugated cardboard and draw a Christmas tree around the top.
Paint the tree, then cut it out

and glue the tree and drawers to a large piece of poster board; cut this out as well

The drawers may be filled with little surprises, such as those presented in this book !

Christmas Cards

easy   inexpensive   2 to 4 hours

Actual size of decorations

Materials

- 1 package of brightly colored construction paper
- scissors or a craft knife
- a hole punch
- white glue
- 2 sheets of tracing paper
- a pencil • a ruler
- paper clips

1 Cut triangles out of the construction paper: ...” x 8” for the tree and the candle, 4” x 8” for the baby bear. Fold each of the cards in two and flatten the crease with a ruler.

2 Using a pencil, trace the silhouette onto the tracing paper. Then trace the silhouette onto the top side of the card. Close the card and secure it with paper clips, then cut out the silhouette from both sides of the card at the same time.

3 Trace other decorations for the card, cut them out, and glue them to the card. Make the Chritmas balls with a hole punch.

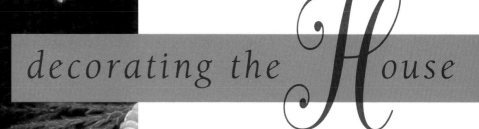

decorating the House

Nothing brings the family together like

decorating the house for Christmas.

All join in to trim the tree, construct the

manger scene, and ready the dining room

for the wonderful feast.

Mini-chimney

easy

inexpensive

1/2 a day

Materials

- 36" x 36" corrugated cardboard
- 2 or 3 big cardboard boxes
- 1 craft knife • scissors
- packing tape
- multi-purpose glue
- a stapler
- tubes of yellow, orange, and brown paint
- a paint brush
- yellow and orange tissue paper

1 Cut out all the pieces of the chimney from the cardboard.

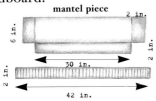

mantel piece
2 in.
6 in.
2 in.
30 in.
2 in.
42 in.

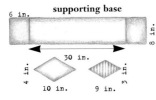

supporting base
6 in.
8 in.
30 in.
4 in.
10 in.
9 in.
3 in.

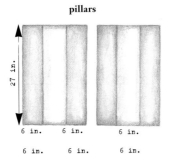

pillars
27 in.
6 in.   6 in.   6 in.

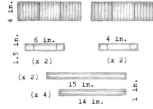

6 in.   6 in.   6 in.
4 in.

6 in.   4 in.
1.5 in.
(x 2)   (x 2)

(x 2)   15 in.
(x 4)   14 in.   1 in.

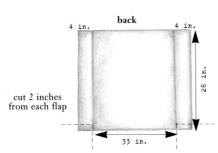

back
4 in.   4 in.
26 in.
cut 2 inches from each flap
33 in.

2 Fold the pillars and support the back with strips of cardboard taped to the back.

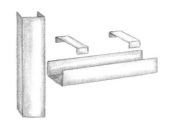

3 Assemble the mantel piece with tape, then glue the strip of corrugated cardboard around the edges. Glue the mantle piece onto the supporting base. Then glue the ensemble onto the pillars.

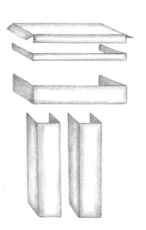

4 Attach the back of the chimney. Tape the flaps behind the pillars.

5 Staple or glue the decorative accents onto the mantel and pillars.

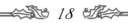

Trace and cut out the outline of flames on a piece of cardboard. Paint and let dry. Cut out strips of tissue paper and glue on to simulate flames.

Cut out a cardboard base. Glue it onto the front of the flames. Cut out logs, paint them, and glue them to the base.

Note
Use one large cardboard box to make the base of the chimney and the pillars.

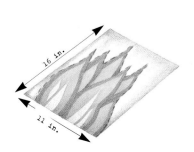

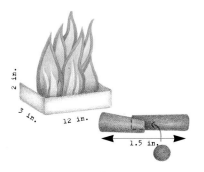

Pretzel Wreath

easy   reasonable   2 to 4 hours

Materials

- a Styrofoam wreath
- assorted sizes of pretzels
- scissors • multi-purpose glue
- a roll of red or green crepe paper • 3 yards of plaid, and gingham or red and green striped ribbon
- a ruler

1 Cut off a long piece of crepe paper. Wind it tightly around the Styrofoam wreath covering it completely. Glue the end.

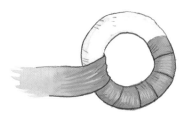

2 Wind the ribbon around the wreath while regularly threading through different sizes of pretzels; finish with a knot.

Tie a bundle of pretzel sticks up in a ribbon and tie them to the wreath. Tie ribbon around pretzels and tie them to the wreath.

3 Attach 4" of ribbon to hang the wreath vertically, or tie ribbons to the top side in order to hang it like a chandelier.

Note:
You can also make a mini-wreath with a large pretzel ring.

Rustic Wreath

easy

inexpensive

2 to 4 hours

1 Combine a cup of salt, a cup and a half of cold water, then two cups of flour in a mixing bowl. If the dough is too dry or too moist, add water or flour. Knead until supple.

2 Roll out two 16" coils of dough and twist them together. Close the ring and seal the end with water. Make another smaller wreath.

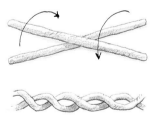

3 Shape the decorative pieces. "Glue" poppy seeds, salt, or sesame seeds onto the wreath by moistening the dough. Put the decorations on after having flattened them to the proper dimensions, apply water to the back of each piece to make it stick.

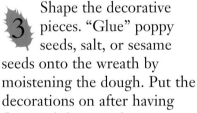

leaf

slash marks

crisscross and reattach each end

pretzel

flower

loaf of bread

slash marks

Materials
- wheat flour
- table salt • water
- a bowl • a cup • a knife
- a rolling pin • grains: poppy seeds, sesame seeds, and kosher salt
- aluminum foil
- a small bowl of water
- a paint brush
- plaid ribbon
- glue

4 Let the wreaths air dry or bake them in a 200° F oven, monitor cooking time. Tie them together with a piece of ribbon and hang them up.

Note:
You can paint the wreath or color the dough by adding food coloring or add a powdered spice (curry, paprika...).

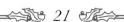

Paper Chains

easy   inexpensive   about 1 hour

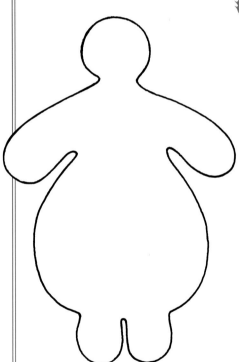

1 Trace and cut out a strip of paper 4" tall; the length should be 3" times the number of shapes wanted. For a chain of 5 shapes you need 15" of paper. Fold the strip like an accordion every 3", or every 6" to make a chain with double shapes.

2 Trace the chosen pattern on one side and secure the folded paper with a paper clip. Cut out the traced image being careful not to cut the hands or the edges of the hearts which serve as the links of the chain.

3 Unfold and decorate the chain by gluing seeds, leaves, or grains to it.

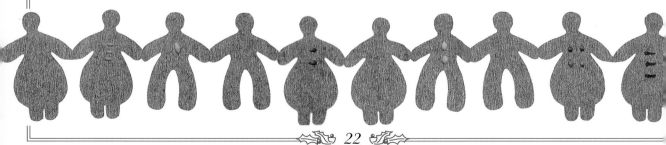

Materials

- craft knife
- crepe paper
- grains, seeds, berries, whole spices...
- thumbtacks or double-sided tape
- a pencil
- a ruler • scissors
- white glue
- paper clips

Note:

When tracing the pattern onto the paper accordion, make sure that the line of the hands or the hearts doesn't go outside of the paper. Hang the paper chain on a wall, a chimney, around a chandelier; use tape or thumbtacks. You can create other patterns: stars, Christmas trees, holly...

Fragant Garlands

 easy   inexpensive   about 1 hour

1 Loop a piece of string through all of the items. Pierce a hole through the tops of the frosted lady fingers with a needle. Loop a piece of string through the holes. Tie all the items along the string, alternating items and lengths of string. Decorate with gingham ribbon.

2 Arrange three vanilla pods or cinnamon sticks in a cross or star shape. Tie them together with a string.

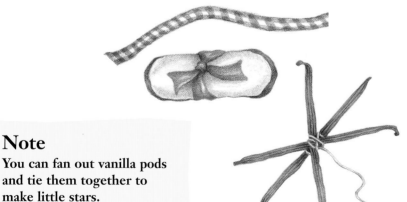

Note
You can fan out vanilla pods and tie them together to make little stars.

Materials
- anise pods
- vanilla pods
- cinnamon sticks
- licorice sticks
- frosted lady finger cookies
- string
- red embroidery thread
- 1 yard of gingham ribbon
- scissors
- cookie cutters

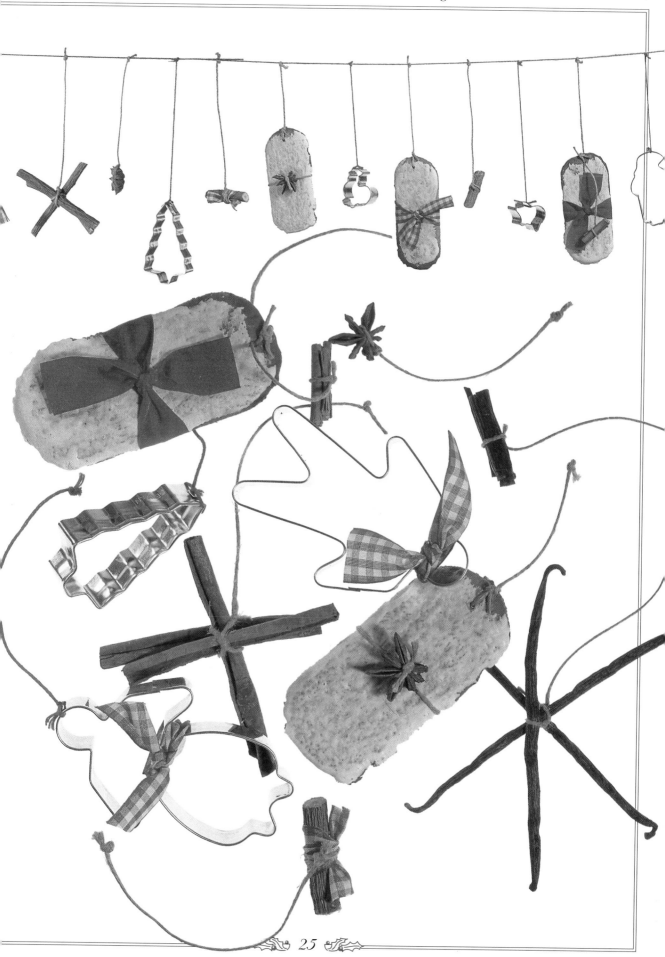

Grain and Legume Ornaments

easy

inexpensive

2 to 4 hours

1 Using a paint brush, coat the surface of the ball with glue. Apply the pieces of grain very close together, covering the surface of the ball completely. Do not press the pieces in too hard. Let it dry thoroughly.

3 Tie raffia around the ball and hang it. Leave 4" free with which to form a loop.

2 Stick a wooden skewer or a pencil into the ball and apply varnish with a paint brush. Let dry.

Note:
The varnish is not obligatory but it gives a shiny appearance and protects the surface of the ornament.

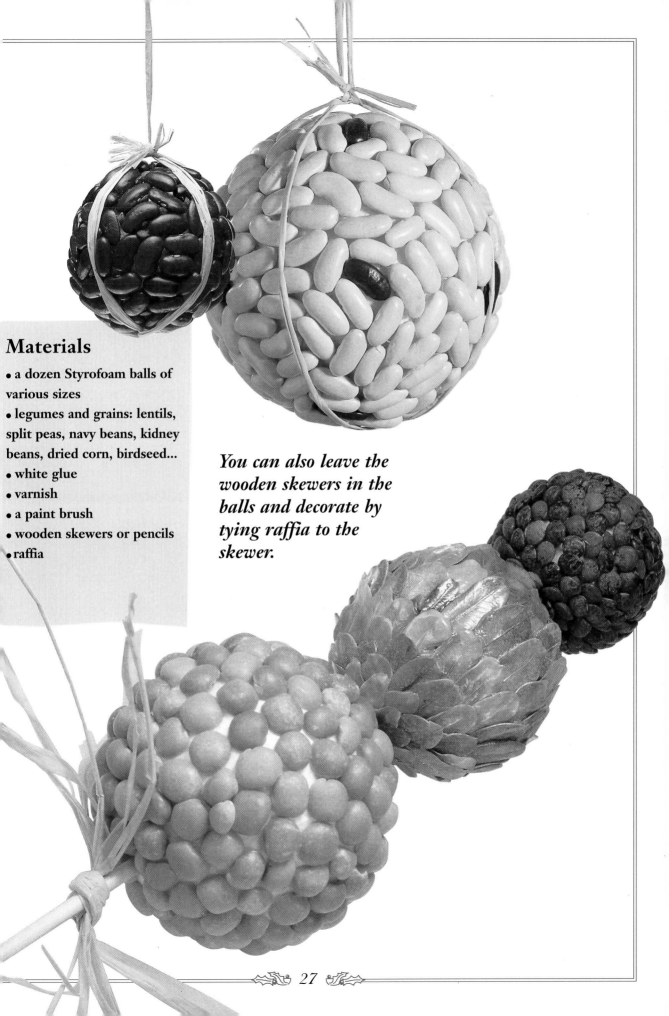

Materials

- a dozen Styrofoam balls of various sizes
- legumes and grains: lentils, split peas, navy beans, kidney beans, dried corn, birdseed...
- white glue
- varnish
- a paint brush
- wooden skewers or pencils
- raffia

You can also leave the wooden skewers in the balls and decorate by tying raffia to the skewer.

Multicolored Christmas Balls

easy   inexpensive   2 to 4 hours
                                   + 24 hours drying time

Materials

- an old newspaper
- wallpaper paste
- a teaspoon
- 1/2 a bowl of water
- a wooden spoon • wire or paper clips • pliers
- assorted colors of paint
- a paint brush • varnish
- adhesive tape

Preparing the glue

With a wooden spoon, mix about two teaspoonfuls of powdered glue in a half a bowl of water. The glue should be rather thick.

Make a paper ball out of newspaper. Make a hanging loop with wire or with a paper clip. Tape it to the paper ball.

Cut out paper strips from the newsprint, making each about 2.5"x1". Dip them one by one into the glue and completely cover the ball, smoothing it out with your fingers as you go.

To decorate, make little paper balls, or twist small paper strips and attach them to the larger, wet paper ball.

4 Let the balls hang to dry, then paint them. Finish with a coat of varnish.

Felt Cushion Ornaments

 easy   affordable   2 to 4 hours

Holly Leaves

1 Draw the holly leaves onto a piece of dark green felt 3"x6", fold it in half and secure it closed with paper clips. Cut out the leaves with pinking shears

3 Cut out two smaller leaves of light green felt, glue them to the second form, and add three red berries.

4 Glue the edges of the first form and attach the second decorated form. Let glue dry.

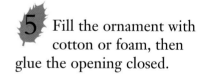

2 Cut out a 4"x1/2" strip of felt and make a loop and glue it to one of the forms.

5 Fill the ornament with cotton or foam, then glue the opening closed.

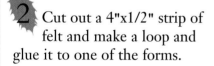

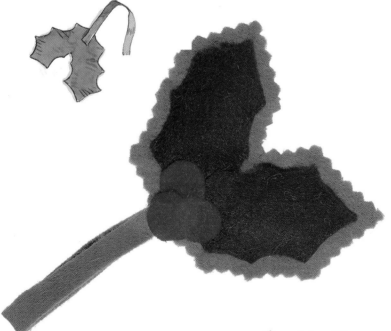

You may design other felt ornaments following the same methods given.

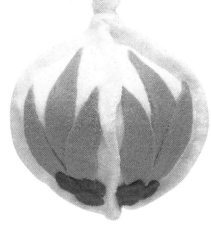

Flower

1 Cut out a 10"x3" strip of felt. Draw and cut out 4 ovals. Draw and cut out four flowers, and leaves smaller than the oval base.

2 Glue the decorations to the ovals and let dry. Cut out a strip of felt, make a loop, and glue it to the inside of one of the ovals.

3 Glue the edges of the ovals together one at a time, leave the last and first edges unglued. Fill the ball and then glue the opening closed.

Materials

- sheets of felt in dark green, light green, red, brown, white and yellow • scissors
- pinking shears
- white glue
- ball-point pen
- cotton or foam
- paper clips

Clay Christmas Figurines

intermediate   reasonable   about 1/2 a day

Santa Claus

1 Roll out a ball of red clay and two smaller balls of pink and white clay, then prepare the pieces as pictured below.

2 Build the body with a ball of aluminum foil, cover it with red clay: the figure is lighter and you save on clay. Flatten the base of the body. Attach the white cuff, pressing lightly to secure it.

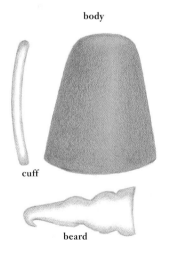

body

cuff

beard

3 Attach the arms to the body, then round out the shoulders. Attach the hands. Attach the cuffs to the wrist.

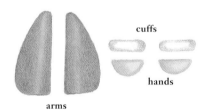

cuffs

hands

arms

4 To form the eyes, poke two holes into the large pink ball with a toothpick. Attach the nose and ears. Place the head on the body, then add the beard and mustache.

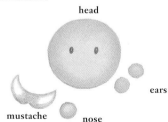

head

mustache

nose

ears

5 Make an indention in the cap. Attach the white pompon to the top of the cap and the white cuff to the base. Put the hat on the head, then incline it towards the front.

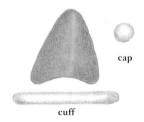

cap

cuff

6 Poke a hole in the hat with help of a needle or gently insert a paper clip into the head.

7 Bake it. Thread a string through the hole or paper clip to hang.

Medallion

1 Roll out several red, yellow, and orange balls.

2 Role out a thin and long coil of red clay. Surround it with three thinner yellow coils of clay, then roll it all up in a thick sheet of orange clay. Roll together to form one large coil.

3 Cut three sections of the same length. Twist them carefully, stick them together and roll out a new roll.

4 Cut into slices. Flatten the pieces out with your palm. Cut out medallions using a small glass.

5 Before baking the figure, pierce a hole through the top.

Note:
Wash hands when changing colors. Make light green clay mixing dark green & white, pink clay mixing red & white. Before working knead until smooth. Varnish after baking & cooling.

Materials
- Small blocks of polymer modeling clay in black, green, blue and red • 1 medium block of white clay • 2 medium blocks of yellow clay • a rolling pin • a craft knife • a tooth pick • a ruler • double-sided tape • paper clips • a small glass • a small cup • a needle • silver or gold wire • aluminum foil • a cookie sheet

Baking
Place clay figurines on aluminum foil and place on a cookie sheet. Bake about 15min. at 275° F. Attach double-sided tape to the back of each figurine.

Glazed Clay Crèche

easy

inexpensive

2 to 4 hours
24 hours drying
time

1 Model the people, the manger, and the animals

2 Form the wells by piling stone shaped clay pieces on top of one another while forming a circle. For the wall, roll out a sheet of clay about 1/3" thick. Cut stone forms into the clay using a knife. Curve the wall and add several loose clay stones to give it the appearance of a ruin.

3 Let it dry for 24 hours, varnish the people and the animals.

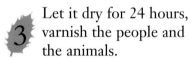

4 Sprinkle a bed of sand for the floor of the Crèche and a small pile of straw for Jesus. Install the figures. Decorate the crèche with cactus.

Materials

- **2 lbs. of red clay**
- **glaze** • **a paint brush**
- **a knife** • **straw** • **sand**
- **small cactus**

Note:
With the remaining clay, you can model the wise men, sheperds, and other crèche characters.

Clay Crèche Characters

intermediate   reasonable   about a day

Gaspar

1 The head

Roll out two small balls of skin-colored clay, one for the head and one smaller for the nose. Attach the nose, pressing lightly. Using a toothpick poke two holes for the eyes and make indentions for the eyebrows and mouth. Flatten a small ball of pink clay and cut out the checks using a pen cap.

2 The body

Form an orange cone about 2" high, flatten the base to stabilize the body. Make an indention around the base with a toothpick. Roll out a small coil of skin-colored clay and cut off the ends. Place the neck on the body, stick a toothpick down through the center and stick the head on the remaining end.

3 The hair, beard, and mustache

Roll out two thin, very small coils of brown clay. Model the mustache and attach it under the nose.

4 The coat

Roll out a ball of orange clay with the rolling pin. Cut out a rectangle and make two channels from end to end with a toothpick. Attach the coat around the center of the body.

5 The necklace

Roll out small balls of red and yellow clay. Cut out two rectangles of the same size, then two v-shaped collars. Attach the red collar over the shoulders and chest, then place the yellow one on top. Decorate with seven small red balls, pierce holes in the centers with toothpicks.

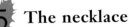

6 The hands

Flatten a skin colored ball of clay. Cut out a circle with the pen cap. Cut it in half. Attach the hands to the sides of the body.

Note:
See note in the Clay Christmas Figurines. You can use a garlic press to make the hair.

7 The cape

Roll out a red and yellow ball of clay. Use the small bowl to cut out yellow circles for the cape and trim. Cut them in half with a ruler. Attach the trim to the cape, gently drape the cape over the figure and lightly press folds.

Materials

- blocks of polymer clay in purple, pink, green, blue, black, red and 2 medium blocks of polymer in yellow and white • See pp. 34, 35 for the remaining materials.

shoulder collar

coat trim

Balthazar　　**Melchior**　　turban

8 The crown

Roll out a small yellow ball. Cut out a rectangle, and the points of the crown. Seal the edges together and place it on the king's head.

headdress

hair

Mary　　**Joseph**　　cloak

Model the other figures just like Gaspar.

Crèche Figurines to Color

easy   reasonable   2 to 4 hours

Head

1 Roll out skin-colored balls of clay 1" in diameter, 3/4" for the children and 1/2" for baby Jesus.

2 Flatten out thin disks of clay for the hair. Cut out bangs with a knife. Roll out small balls for the nose. Model the mouth, eyes, beard, mustache and Jesus' cheeks. Attach parts to the heads.

Materials

• Small blocks of modeling clay in skin-colored, black, brown, yellow, red, blue, and green
• all-purpose glue
• acrylic paint, markers, or crayons
• paint brushes • scissors • a knife • 2 sheets of tag board
• a pencil
• tracing paper • a toothpick
• a compass • a ruler

3 Model cones from the skin-colored clay. Attach the heads on top, pressing lightly.

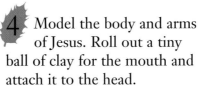

4 Model the body and arms of Jesus. Roll out a tiny ball of clay for the mouth and attach it to the head.

5 Bake them as you did the Clay Christmas Figurines.

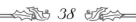

Joseph

Collar

Mary

Collar

Shephard

Collar

Body

1 Trace the body onto the tag board

2 For each figure draw arms, hands, clothing as well as the gifts. Paint or color each body and let it dry.

3 Cut out and glue body around the clay cone.

Angel

Collar

Wings

Children

Collar

Collar

Collar

Collar

Collar

Collar

Collar

Collar

3 in.

1 in.

3 in.

1/2 in.

Three Wise Men

Stencil Tablecloth

intermediate

rather
expensive

1 day

Note:
Adjust the position of the tablecloth to print at different angles.
Let each stencil dry before beginning the next one.
Hide stains with extra designs.
Wash your hands regularly

1 Trace the stencil pattern onto the piece of cardboard or sheet of plastic; adapt the size of the stencil according to that of the tablecloth. Cut out the images with a craft knife.

2 Place the tablecloth on a large flat work surface; protect the surface with old newspaper. Secure the tablecloth with straight pins: You may also decorate the base of the tablecloth.

3 Choose a portion of the tablecloth and protect the other areas by covering with adhesive tape.

4 Coat the brush in paint, wipe off the excess paint with a piece of newspaper. Holding the brush upright, apply the paint in a dabbing motion.
Work color-by-color around the tablecloth.

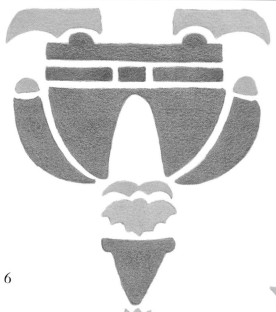

5 Let dry approximately 6 hours.

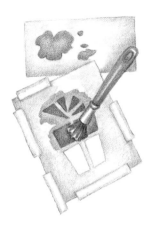

Materials

- a clean white pressed tablecloth
- jars of opaque fabric paint in pink, yellow, white, silver, red, blue, rust, green, and coral
- small stencil brushes (1 for each color)
- adhesive tape
- newspaper
- straight pins
- a thin sheet of plastic or cardboard
- a marker
- a craft knife

Place Mats

easy   reasonable   about one hour

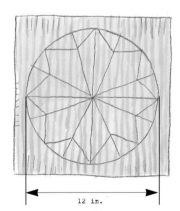

 1 *Mat Designs*

Simple frame
Trace a 12"x16" rectangle on the underside of a piece of corrugated cardboard, then cut it out.

Star design
Draw a star within a 12" diameter circle and cut it out along the outline.

Decorative border
Trace a 12"x16" rectangle onto underside of a piece of corrugated cardboard. Draw the designs for the border within the rectangle. Cut out the mat following the contours of the border.

Materials
- colored corrugated cardboard
- poster board or construction paper in various colors
- scissors
- white glue
- a ruler
- a pencil

12 in.

Decorative Design

2 Trace a 12"x16" rectangle on the underside of a piece of corrugated cardboard. Draw the border designs within the rectangle. Cut out the external rectangle, then cut out the interior following the contours of the border. Glue the border to a simple frame.

Note:
You can create other mat decorations: angels, candles, gifts, stockings, snowmen...

Layered Border

3 Draw designs on the poster board. Cut them out. Before gluing them down arrange the pieces as you want them.

Menus and Napkin Rings

easy   inexpensive   about 1 hour

1 Trace around the cardboard tube every 2". Cut off each section carefully with a craft knife.

2 Cut out a 6"x9" rectangle from the cardboard box. Fold it in half.

3 Iron the fusible web onto the felt.

4 Trace the dimensions of the cardboard rectangle and the rings onto the fusible web. Cut them out with scalloped scissors.

5 Glue the felt, web side, onto the cardboard rectangle and rings pressing it down for several seconds.

6 Cut out green bands of felt 1" in width with the pinking shears. Glue them to the middle of the rings about 2/3 down.

7 Decorate the menu and the ring with decorative pieces cut from the remaining felt, then glue them on.

Note:
Fusible web stiffens fabric which enables one to easily draw on them. It is inexpensive and can be purchased in sewing stores.

8 Cut out white paper the same size as the menu cover, fold it in half and secure it to the menu cover with a thin knotted ribbon. Then all you need to do is write....

Materials

- pinking shears
- cardboard paper towel roll
- 8"x20" of red felt
- 4"x20" of green felt
- sharp scissors
- 8"x20" fusible web
- all-purpose glue
- a craft knife
- an iron
- a ballpoint pen
- a white piece of paper
- 20" of fine green ribbon
- a tape measure

Knife Holders

easy inexpensive about one hour

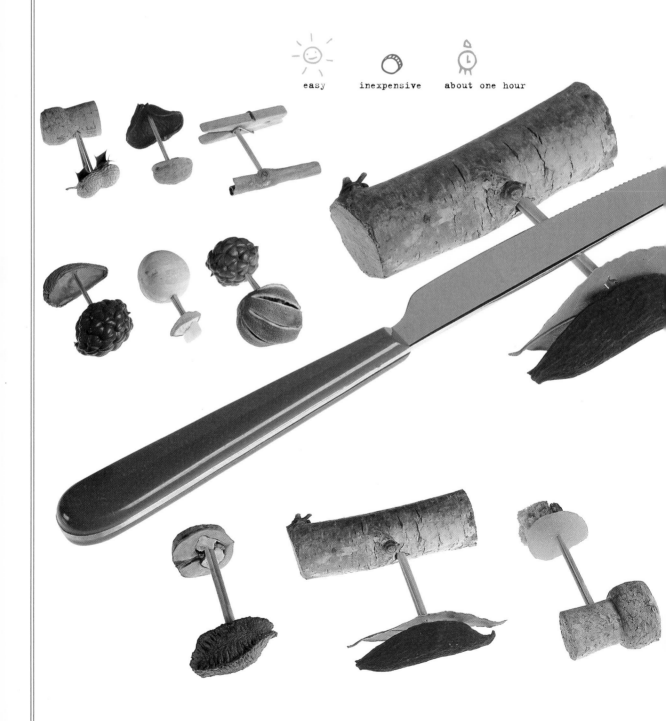

Materials

- objects of nature: dried fruit, nuts, petals, leaves, twigs, etc.
- champagne cork
- wooden tooth picks
- a knife
- a nut cracker
- a clothes pin

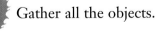

1 Gather all the objects.

2 Sort the objects together according to size, and stick them together using 3-5 toothpicks.

Note:
You can make edible knife holders using sweet items or savory items like cherry tomatoes, cheese cubes, sliced sausage or peppers.

Sculpted Place Cards

easy   inexpensive   2 to 4 hours
24 hours drying
time

1 Model the forms from the wire. Cut out 3"x2" cardboard rectangles for support. Pierce holes in the cardboard to stick forms through and tape them underneath.

2 Prepare the wallpaper paste. Cut out small strips of newspaper. Dip the strips into the glue and paste them onto the form and its base, cover it completely. Shape and smooth with your fingers.

4 Cut out a slit in the base to slide a rectangle of poster board as the name card.

3 Let dry for approximately 24 hours. Paint, then varnish when it has dried.

Note:

To prepare the glue, refer to
page 28, the multi-colored
Christmas Balls

Claire

Catherine

Painted Candle Holders

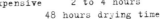

easy   inexpensive   2 to 4 hours
                              48 hours drying time

 **1** Roll the clay out about 1/4" thick.

 3 With the pen cap, remove a piece of clay from the center of each candle holder.
Let them dry for 48 hours.

 2 Using the cutter, press out different shapes.

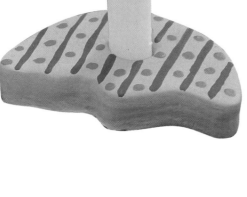

Note:
You can also cut the candle holders out yourself with a craft knife.

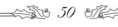

Materials

• 1 lb of air-drying modeling clay
• cookie cutters
• a pen cap
• acrylic paint in red, blue, green, yellow, orange, white.
• a paint brush
• candle sticks
• a rolling pin

4 Apply a prime coat of white paint. Once dry, apply a layer of colored paint, let dry. Paint according to your own taste.

Cookie Cutter Candle Holders

easy   inexpensive   2 to 4 hours

1 Begin with a sheet of wax. Cut out the bases with different cookie cutters.

Materials

- sheets of colored wax
- candle wick
- cookie cutters
- a water bowl

2 Begin with a sheet of wax. For each candle, cut two identical shapes of the same color.

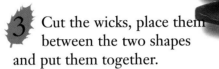

3 Cut the wicks, place them between the two shapes and put them together.

4 Decorate one side of the candle with bits of wax or clay. Attach the form to the base.

Note:

Before beginning, dip the wax in the lukewarm water to make it more malleable.
To adhere two pieces of wax, press them between your fingers. If you cut out pieces of wax with a knife, cut out the two sides of the candle at the same time so they will be identical.

Stained Glass Stencils

intermediate   reasonable   about 1 hour

1 To make the stencil, trace the pattern of the tree and gift onto a sheet of paper and cut them out.

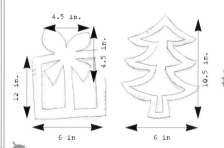

2 Trace the stencil onto the back of the poster board and cut out three times, overlapping each time.

3 Place the stencils onto three different colors of tissue paper and trace. Glue the outer edge of the back of the poster board and paste the tissue paper to it.

4 Cut out small decorative accents and glue them to the tissue paper.

5 Trace the star on poster board and tissue paper, cut out and glue together. Trace the snowflake onto the poster board and cut out. Glue to the center of the star.

Materials

- construction paper in assorted colors
- tissue paper in assorted colors
- scissors or a craft knife
- white glue
- a pencil
- double-sided tape
- 2 pieces of paper
- a ruler

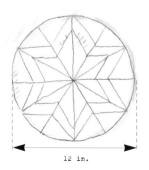

You can also decorate windows or French doors with the stencils.

Votive Stained Glass Stencils

1 Construct the stencil windows following the same techniques as for the window stencils, adapting the height to that of the votive candle holder you wish to decorate.

2 Tape the stencil window to the candle holder with double sided tape.

3 Place a candle in the holder. Attention, the candle needs to be short enough that it won't catch the paper on fire.

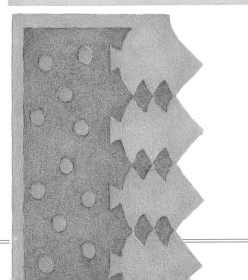

Holiday Windows

easy   inexpensive   about one hour

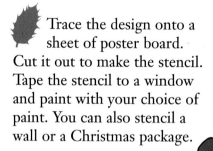

Trace the design onto a
sheet of poster board.
Cut it out to make the stencil.
Tape the stencil to a window
and paint with your choice of
paint. You can also stencil a
wall or a Christmas package.

Materials

- scissors or a craft knife
- a pencil
- poster board
- adhesive tape
- paint
- stencil brush
- artificial snow

little Gifts

Christmas turns everyone into Santa's

helper. All of the planning is secretly

rewarded when the children's eyes widen

and shine as they open their gifts.

Giant Poppers

Note:

Careful not to twist the popper too much when unraveling it. Roll the tubes horizontally with the grain of the crepe paper.

easy

inexpensive

2 to 4 hours

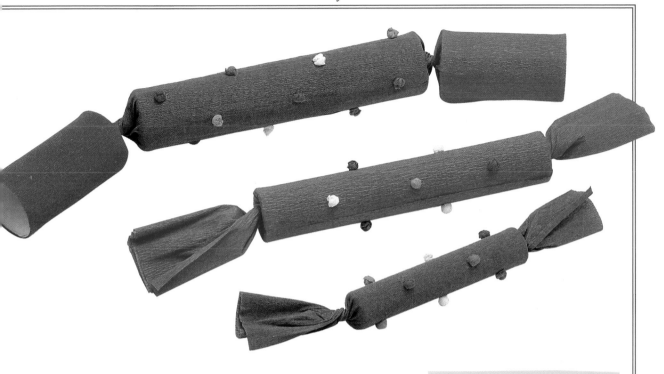

1 Unravel a small popper part-way. Tape it to the inside, middle of the largest tube, tape each string to the inside of both smaller tubes.

2 Cut out a 10"x8" strip and two 6"x6" strips of crepe paper in different colors. Glue the three strips together, largest in the middle, overlapping each about 1/2".

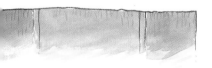

3 Cover the rolls with the crepe paper, leaving a space between each roll. Glue the paper the length of each tube. Let dry.

4 Fill each popper with little surprises before sealing. Decorate them by gluing little paper balls to the larger tube.

Materials

- **paper towel rolls**
- **a pencil**
- **a ruler**
- **scissors**
- **white glue**
- **double sided tape**
- **poppers**
- **little surprises**

Snow Balls

intermediate   reasonable   2 to 4 hours

1 Model a Christmas figurine (not too tall nor too wide for the jar) with assorted colors of modeling clay.

Materials

• small glass jars with lids (baby food, pickle, jelly)
• blocks of polymer clay in black, green, red, white and yellow
• strong glue • artificial Styrofoam snow • see the remainder of materials in the Clay Christmas Figurines (pages 32-33)

2 Form a clay base, assemble and attach the pieces of the figurine to it. Finish by decorating the figurine.

Note:
Refer to the advice given for modeling and baking the Clay Christmas Figurines (pages 32-33).
For the snowman's broom: the handle is a simple toothpick, the straw is made by putting the clay through a garlic press.

3 Bake the clay figurine, then glue it to the lid of the jar.

4 Pour some of the artificial snow into the jar and fill it with water. Gently close the lid...

... seal it tightly and turn it over.

Little Winter Picture Frames

easy   inexpensive   2 to 4 hours

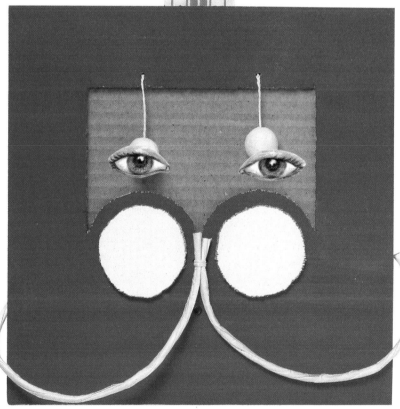

Santa Claus

1 Cut out 2 cardboard squares 8" on the sides and 2 circles of 2" in diameter. Transfer the pattern onto one of the cardboard squares and cut out the window with a sharp craft knife. Using a hole punch pierce two small holes for the eyes, two others for the mustache attachment and a large hole for the mouth. Paint the face and the cheeks. Let dry.

2 Attach the mustache handles in the center hole with string. Stick the knotted end of the string through a Styrofoam ball, thread the other end through an eye hole and secure with a knot. Repeat for the other eye. Glue the cheeks on, then the suspension ribbon, 12" long. Insert a photo of your choice and tape to the back of the frame on with double sided tape.

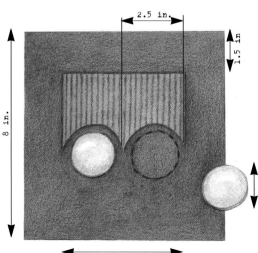

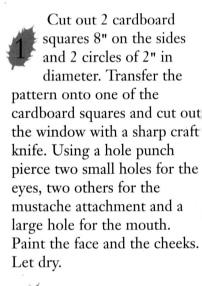

Materials

- 4 cardboard boxes
- a pencil • a ruler
- a hole punch
- wooden skewers
- 36" of wide ribbon
- an eraser • scissors
- white glue • kitchen twine
- 10 Styrofoam balls of assorted sizes • double-sided tape •plastic sack handles

Three Trees

1 Cut out 2 rectangles from the cardboard 8"x6" (cut parallel with the channels of the cardboard). Trace the internal frame on one of these, then cut it out. Paint the cardboard and the Styrofoam balls. Let them dry.

2 Stick the Styrofoam balls onto the wooden skewers to form Christmas trees. Glue confetti made with a hole punch to the cardboard frame, then the suspension ribbon. Place the photo of your choice inside and close the frame. Slide the picks into the channels of the cardboard.

Note:

Stick the Styrofoam balls onto the wooden skewers to paint them.

To make the confetti, flatten the cardboard before sliding it into the hole punch. You can replace the plastic bag handle with string, but you will have to glue it in place.

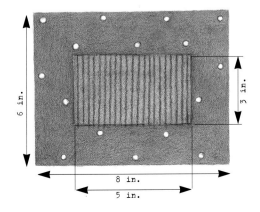

Decorated Mirrors

intermediate   reasonable   about a 1/2 a day

Holly and Mistletoe Wreath

1 Trace the shape of the mirror onto the paper with the marker. Roll out two balls of green clay. Roll one out into a coil about 1/2" thick. Lay it over the circle that you traced.

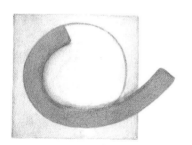

2 Separate the other green ball in half. Mix it with some white clay to make light green clay. Flatten out and shape the balls into strips about 1/8" thick on the aluminum foil.

The roses can be made by cutting thin strips of clay and wrapping them around each other.

3 Cut out the holly and mistletoe leaves. Place them around the circle layering them as you go.

4 Roll out small red and white balls. Place around the wreath.

5 Bake. Glue the wreath to the mirror.

Note:
Refer to the advice given in the Clay Christmas Figurines (pages 32-33).
Stick the hook into the clay before baking.

Moon

1 Trace the shape of the mirror onto the paper.

2 Mold a 3/4 moon out of aluminum foil covering 3/4 of the pattern. knead out some yellow clay and cover the aluminum mold with it. Smooth the surface with your fingers.

3 Mold different facial features and cap. Attach them to the face, use your fingers to refine the features. Bake it and glue it to the mirror.

eye

eye lid

cap

eye brow

mouth

nose

Materials

- Holly: 2 medium blocks of polymer clay, in green, 1 in red, and 1 in white.
- Moon: 2 blocks of yellow clay, 1 block of red clay and a bit of black and white clay
- blank drawing paper
- a marker
- glue • picture frame hooks
- round mirrors • see the rest of the materials in the Clay Christmas Figurines (pages 32-33).

Magnetic Playboard Landscape

intermediate   reasonable   about 1/2 a day

Materials

- a sheet of magnetic board
- 15"x20" piece of double-sided corrugated cardboard
- corrugated cardboard
- cardboard
- glue • 10"x16" piece of contact paper in white and blue • scissors • paper clips
- picture frame hook
- double-sided tape
- magnetic squares • 1 cutter
- a craft knife • a fine point marker. See the materials for papier-mâché in the **Multicolored Christmas Balls** (pp. 28-29)

Figurines

1 Draw and cut out forms from the cardboard. Cover the final forms with papier-mâché add decorative accents and paint them according to the process used for the place cards. (pages 48-49).

2 Glue a small magnet square to each figure.

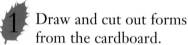

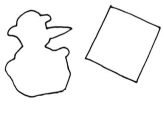 

Playboard

1 Draw and cut out a mountain range from the white contact paper. Secure it with paper clips to the middle of the blue paper and cut off the bottom half.

2 Glue the blue paper to the magnetic board. Position the mountain range on top of the blue paper and glue it down.

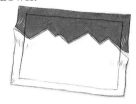

Size up the cardboard rectangle with the magnetic board, cut off the excess cardboard and glue together.

3 Cut out strips of cardboard about 2"x20" and 2"x16". Glue them one after the other to the edges of the landscape. Bevel the corners. Glue 1"x20" and 1"x16" strips of corrugated cardboard on top of that.

4 Attach the hanging hook to the landscape with double-sided adhesive tape.

Theme Notebooks

easy   reasonable   2 to 4 hours

Materials

- **sheets of foam in assorted colors**
- **1 or more notebooks**
- **craft glue**
- **scissors**
- **a pencil**
- **hole punch**

1 Open the notebook. Glue a sheet of foam to the cover of the notebook. Cut off the overlap with scissors.

2 Trace a square or rectangle with straight or wavy sides inside a sheet of foam. It should be smaller than the notebook. Cut out and glue the motifs to the center of the notebook.

You can also decorate a recipe book, a journal, or a photo album...

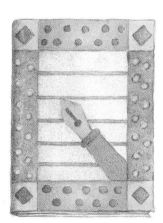

3 Trace and cut out other designs in different colors of foam. The dots are made with a hole punch. Glue the pieces one at a time onto the notebook. Let dry.

Note:
To give a refined touch to the notebook, glue two pieces of ribbon to each side of the cover. Tie together in a nice bow.

Jumping Santa Claus

advanced

reasonable

2 to 4 hours

1 *Head*

Flatten a small ball of skin-colored clay and cut out the head with a small glass (2" to 3" in diameter). Press a small ball of skin-colored clay into the center for the nose. Cut out cheeks and ears with a pen cap. Model other pieces. Attach the following by pressing gently: cheeks, eyes, cap trim, pompon, ears, eyebrows, mustache, and beard.

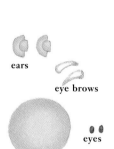

ears

eye brows

eyes

nose

cheeks

cap

mustache

beard

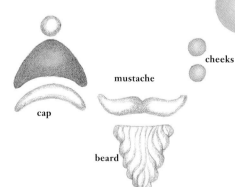

Materials

- small blocks of polymer clay in yellow, green, brown, and pink
- medium blocks of skin-colored and white clay
- 2 medium blocks of red clay
- 12" of thin cord
- See the remaining materials in the Christmas figurines (pages 32-33).

2 *Arms and Legs*

Roll out a sheet of red clay 1/4" thick. Cut out the arms and legs with a knife. Roll a small green ball of clay and cut in half for the feet. Model and attach the cuffs, hands, thumbs, feet, and pompons. Pierce holes in the arms and legs with a ball point pen.

Note:

If you want to hang the Santa, stick a hook into the cap before cooking.

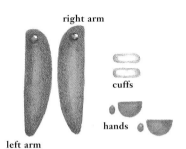

right arm

cuffs

hands

left arm

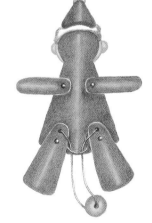

4 *Assembly*

Bake each part separately. Break a toothpick into 4-1" pieces. Stick a toothpick through each arm of the decorated body.

buttons

feet

legs

3 *Body*

Roll out a sheet of red clay 1/4" thick. Cut out the two bodies. Superimpose them and pierce holes in them. Model and attach the coat trim, the belt, and the belt buckle. Model a small bead of clay

3/4" diameter. Pierce through it with a toothpick. Do not attach it to the body. Attach the head to the body, then add the beard and mustache.

Thread the clay bead onto a piece of string and thread the string through the holes in the legs and tie a knot in the end. Stick toothpicks through each leg. Attach the other side of the body. Squish little clay balls into the holes to hide them.

Snowman Pajama Carrier

easy   reasonable   2 to 4 hours

1 Fold the terry cloth in half and pin down. Position the plates to draw the snowman. On the red felt, draw two circles for the cheeks, six circles for the buttons and the hands.

3 Sew together the two sides of the snowman, leaving a 6" opening at the bottom. Hem the opening. Sew on the button eyes.

Easy nightcap to make:
Cut out a 25"x30" triangle of red felt. Glue the long sides together. Cut out a 2"x12" rectangle of the felt for the tassel. Fringe the rectangle. Glue the top and wind it around a piece of string, then attach the string to the tip of the cap.

4 Glue on all the pieces, stuff the head and tie the scarf around the neck.

2 Cut out the snowman and the other pieces leaving a 1/2" margin. Don't forget a red rectangle for the scarf and an orange for the nose. Cut out freckles with the hole punch.

Note:
To help trace the cheeks and buttons use round objects such as a glass, a plastic tube, a bottle...

Materials

- white terry cloth • red, green, and orange felt (or fabric) • a fine point marker
- fabric glue • a needle or sewing machine
- straight pins
- red and white thread
- a small plate
- a larger plate
- for the head: old rags, cotton or foam
- 2 red buttons

Imprinted Gift Wrapping

easy

reasonable

about 1/2 a day

The stamps

1 Trace the designs on the foam. Cut them out carefully with scissors or a craft knife.

2 Glue the foam designs onto a sturdy support, made by gluing six small cardboard rectangles together. Let dry.

Note:

Clean the paintbrush and stamps before changing colors. Dry them off with a rag. Do not dilute the paint. It should be rather thick. It will dry quickly, but you can use a blow-dryer to speed of drying time.

Tags and strings

1 Cut out 3"x2" rectangles with pinking shears. Punch a hole in the corner. Tie the tag to the package with about 8" of gold string.

2 Take a long strip of crepe paper and roll it between your fingers to form a solid twisted cord. Cut into lengths of about 36".

Stamping

1 Apply paint to the surface of the stamp with a small paint brush. Test the stamp on a page of newspaper to determine how much paint to use.

2 Stamp the paper and the tags. Paint borders on some of them.

Materials

- white construction paper
- ecru and white craft paper
- rolls of crepe paper in various colors • a hole punch
- pinking shears
- yellow, orange, red, pink, green, blue, and gold paint
- small paint brush
- pointed scissors
- transparent glue
- sheets of foam
- ball point pen • sturdy cardboard • gold thread

treats for the Table

In the warmth

of the holiday season, the gifts of love,

imagination, and traditional offerings

combine to create a beautiful feast

both for the eyes and the palate.

Sweet Treats

Fruit Faces

easy   reasonable   about 2 hours

1 Prepare balls of almond paste of various colors: create different colored paste by kneading in drops of food coloring.

2 Flatten the balls of paste into oval, round, or profile shapes.
A dry apricot or a date may also serve as a head.

3 Vary the colors and materials to create silly faces.

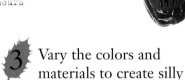

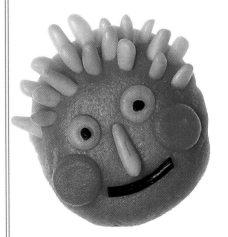

Ingredients

- green, red, and yellow food coloring
- white almond paste (marzipan)
- dried fruit: prunes, dates, apricots, raisins, pinenuts, sugar sequins, sugar sprinkles, and silver candies
- licorice strings

Christmas Sugar Cookies

easy   inexpensive   2 to 4 hours

1 Blend the butter and sugar together in a mixing bowl, using your fingers. Add the flour and baking soda.

2 Break an egg into a bowl and beat with a fork. Stir in the milk. Add this to the flour mixture. Let chill for one hour.

3 Dust the work surface with flour. Roll out the dough and cut out the cookies.

4 Place cookies on an ungreased cookie sheet and bake in a 373°F for 15 to 20 minutes.

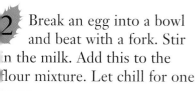

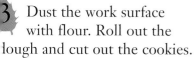

5 Mix powdered sugar and egg white in a bowl. Separate the frosting into different bowls, one for each color and add various food colorings.

6 Frost the cookies. Decorate the cookies according to taste.

Ingredients
makes 25 cookies
- green, red, and yellow food coloring • 2 cups flour
- 1/2 cup butter
- 1 cup sugar
- 1 egg • 1/2 teaspoon baking powder • 1/4 cup milk
- 4 oz. white icing
- sprinkles, sequins and various other sugar decorations

Materials
- cookie cutters
- mixing bowls • wooden spoon • a bowl • a fork
- a rolling pin
- a knife

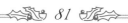

Marzipan Yule Log Cake

intermediate   reasonable   2 to 4 hours

Note:
The cake decorations may also be made of almond paste. You can substitute the apricot jam and the almond paste with chocolate icing.

Ingredients
make 6 servings

- 4 eggs
- 2 cups powdered sugar
- 2 cups flour • a teaspoon of baking powder • 8 oz. almond paste (marzipan)
- green, red, yellow, and brown food coloring
- silver sugar candy pearls
- butter
- apricot jam

Cake Roll

1 Separate the egg white from the yolks. Whip the yolks with the sugar in a bowl.

2 When the mixture becomes white and frothy, gradually add the flour and baking powder.

3 Beat the whites until they are stiff. Gently fold them into the mixture.

4 Grease the pan with butter. Pour in the batter. Bake for 10 minutes in a 450°F oven.

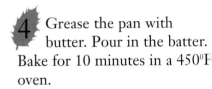

5 When the cake is done turn it over onto a sugared surface and remove the pan. Cover with a damp towel and let cool.

6 Spread a layer of jam on the cake and carefully roll it up.

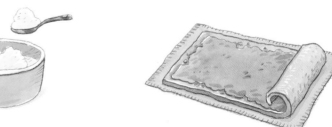

Decorations

1 Take two thirds of the almond paste. Color it [b]rown by kneading in food [c]oloring. Smooth it out and [c]over the cake with it. Using a [k]nife cut in the bark design [an]d let harden.

2 Color two large balls of almond paste red, one [p]ink, and a small one blue. [L]eave one white. Model skiers [o]f different sizes.

3 Color a large ball of green paste. Flatten it out [to] a 1/4" thick sheet. [U]sing a cookie cutter or a [k]nife cut out 8 stars increasing [in] size. Pile them on top of

one another alternating the rays as you go. Finish with a small cone for the top of the tree. Decorate with silver sugar candy pearls.

4 Cut out holly leaves and cut in veins with a knife.

5 Place the skiers and the tree on the top of the cake. Stick the holly leaves and holly berries onto the sides of the cake.

Materials

- **3 star cookie cutters of various sizes**
- **a sheet cake pan**
- **two mixing bowls**
- **a wooden spoon**
- **an electric mixer**
- **a clean dish towel**

Ginger Bread House

intermediate

affordable

approx.
half a day

Ingredients
- slices of ginger bread cake or graham crackers
- 4 oz. icing
- an egg white
- lady finger cookies
- 8 oz. almond paste(marzipan)
- food coloring
- sugar sequins
- silver sugar candy pearls

1 In a mixing bowl, mix the icing with the egg white. This will serve as the glue. Form the foundation of the house by "gluing" slices of ginger bread together.

2 Use 10 slices to build the walls. Cut two slices of bread sideways to build the gables.

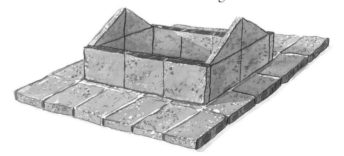

3 Build two similar walls with gables in the interior of the house to support the roof.

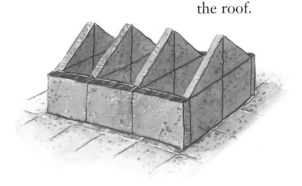

4 To build the roof, start by gluing slices of bread on top of the framework. Then, starting at the base of the roof, glue on lady fingers to serve as tiles. Let dry 1 to 2 hours.

5 Model decorations and characters from the almond paste, using a rolling pin and a knife. Simulate snow with the icing mixture.

Materials

- star cookie cutters
- a small bowl
- a wooden spoon
- a basting brush
- a knife
- a rolling pin

King Cake

Ingredients
makes 6 servings

- 3 sheets of puff pastry
- 2 eggs • 2 cups almond flour
- 1 1/2 cups butter
- 1 1/2 cups sugar
- 1 tablespoon of flour
- crystallized fruit

easy

reasonable

about 1 hour

1 Cream sugar and butter together in a mixing bowl, using a blender.

2 Add the egg, flour, and almond flour and mix until smooth.

3 Unroll a sheet of puff pastry onto a buttered baking sheet. Spread the almond creme onto the pastry sheet leaving a 1" edge. Moisten the edge with a basting brush.

4 Place the second sheet of dough on top and seal together by crimping the edges with a fork.

5 Unroll the third sheet of dough. Cut out the facial features, then place them on top of the cake. Brush the top of cake with egg yolk. Decorate with crystallized fruit, then bake it for 20 to 25 minutes in a preheated 350ºF oven.

Materials

- a wooden spatula • a knife
- a mixing bowl • a basting brush • a fork

King Cake Figurines

easy   reasonable   about one hour

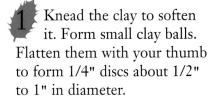

1 Knead the clay to soften it. Form small clay balls. Flatten them with your thumb to form 1/4" discs about 1/2" to 1" in diameter.

2 Model the details with small pieces of clay. Use your imagination to create many different figurines. Bake them on low heat for 20 minutes.

Materials

- small blocks of polymer clay in various colors
- a knife

Note:
Bake the cake and the figurines separately. Place the figurines into the cake after it has cooled.

celebrating with the Family

Christmas gatherings bring the warm

feeling of love, togetherness, and family.

Prolong the joy and excitement of the

celebration by sharing in holiday games,

singing Christmas carols and telling

traditional Christmas stories.

Games for the Entire Family

Funny Snowmen

2 dice, 1 large ball and one small ball of white clay (or potatoes), a match, two whole cloves, 3 coffee beans, and a red ribbon.

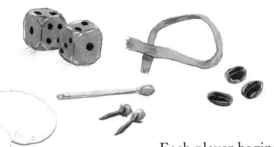

Each player begins with his or her pieces in front of him. To begin the game, the first player rolls the dice. The player must roll a combination of the following: 5= the head, 8= the broom, 9= the scarf, double 2= an eye, double 3= a button. If the player doesn't get one of these combinations, he or she passes the dice to next player. Note: if the player rolls a double 1, he or she must take off a body part. If a player rolls double six, he or she may put on two body parts. The first player to complete his or her snowman wins the game.

Wacky Christmas Stories

Come up with a list of traditional Christmas characters such as, a wise man, the innkeeper, Santa Claus, Mary, an angel, Joseph, a shepherd etc. and write them on little strips of paper. Someone begins by telling a famous story: the story of the three pigs, or Little Red Riding Hood, for example. After a few minutes, the player stops and passes to the next player who chooses another piece of paper and continues the story integrating the character he or she chose. This continues until all of the papers have been chosen. The last person should finish this bizarre story with the original ending of the story.

Variation : A player begins a story with the words "Once upon a time on Christmas Day...." He or she should stop at an exciting moment and throw an orange to another player. This person should continue the story integrating a new character.

Christmas Charades

Draw a game board with numbered squares onto a large piece of paper, alternate the colors: a red square, a green square, a white square, a red square etc.

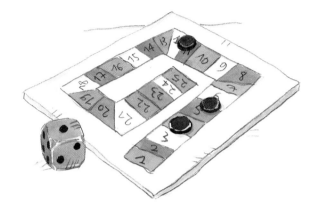

Play in pairs or groups of three. Someone not playing this round prepares a list of five words, five characters, and three songs to guess, keeping with a Christmas theme. Each team throws the dice on his or her turn and advances that number of squares. The red square equals a word, green square a person, and white square a song. One of the players from the team acts out the word, person, or song by miming or singing as long as the hour glass runs. If his or her teammate guesses correctly, the player may take another turn. Beware that rolling a one means that you have to back track three spaces, a six means you have to give up your turn. The first team to reach the 25th square wins.

Variation : with the same list, but without the game board, pick a player from the group to mime or sing in front of the group. The first to guess correctly takes his or her place, and the game continues.

Santa Pin-up Puzzle

Cut out two identical cardboard figures of Santa Claus. Attach one to the wall. The other is colored and cut into separate parts (head, beard, arm, belt, ...) which are distributed to the players. For each turn, blindfold the player and spin him or her around several times. The player should then attempt to pin the body part on the correct area of the body. This one is sure to get a lot of laughs!

Songs

Jingle bells, jingle bells
Jingle all the way!
O what fun it is to ride
In a one-horse open sleigh!

Angels we have heard on high
Sweetly singing o'er the plain
And the mountains in reply
Echoing their sweet refrain.
Gloria in excelsis Deo!

O Christmas Tree

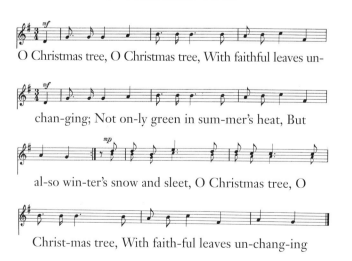

O Christmas tree, O Christmas tree, With faithful leaves un-

chan-ging; Not on-ly green in sum-mer's heat, But

al-so win-ter's snow and sleet, O Christmas tree, O

Christ-mas tree, With faith-ful leaves un-chang-ing

Away in a manger

No crib for a bed
The little Lord Jesus lay down His sweet head
The stars in the sky looked down where He lay.
The little Lord Jesus, asleep on the hay.

Silent Night, Holy Night

All is calm, all is bright
Round yon virgin, mother and child
Holy infant, so tender and mild
Sleep in heavenly peace.
Sleep in heavenly peace.

The First Noel

The first No-el, the angel did say, Was to

cer-tain poor shepherds in fields as they lay; In fields where

they lay keep-ing their sheep, On a cold winter's night that

was so deep. No-el No-el, No-el,

Born is the King of Is-ra-el.

Deck the halls with boughs of holly

Fa-la la-la la, la la la la!
'Tis the season to be jolly! Fa-la la . . .
Don we now our gay apparel
Fa-la la . . .
Troll the ancient Yuletide carol
Fa-la la-la la, la la la la!

While shepherds watched their flocks by night

All seated on the ground,
The angel of the Lord came down
And glory shone around.

We three kings of orient are

Bearing gifts we traverse afar
Field and fountain moor and mountain
Following yonder star
O! Star of wonder, Star of night
Star with royal beauty bright
Westward leading, still proceeding
Guide us to thy perfect light.

Stories to Read or Tell

 ## The Night before Christmas
by Clement Clark Moore

'Twas the night before Christmas, when all through the house not a creature was stirring, not even a mouse;
The stockings were hung by the chimney with care, in the hope that St. Nicholas soon would be there;
The children were nestled all snug in their beds, while visions of sugar plums danced in their heads...

 ## The Little Match Seller
by Hans Christian Andersen

It was terribly cold and nearly dark on Christmas Eve, and the snow was falling fast. In the cold and darkness, a poor little girl, with bare head and naked feet, roamed through the streets selling matches. No one had bought anything from her the whole day, nor had anyone given her even a penny. Her little hands were almost frozen with the cold. Ah! perhaps a burning match might do some good...

 ## The Fir Tree
by Hans Christian Andersen

A small fir tree dreamt about growing tall and old and leaving his home in the forest. Finally, one day in December, a woodcutter cut him down and carried him away. The journey was very unpleasant, but he soon found himself being brought into a house and placed in the middle of a warm living room...